What Are
Inclined Planes?

by Helen Frost

Consulting Editor: Gail Saunders-Smith, Ph.D.

Consultant: Philip W. Hammer, Ph.D.
Assistant Director of Education
American Institute of Physics

Pebble Books

an imprint of Capstone Press
Mankato, Minnesota

Pebble Books are published by Capstone Press
151 Good Counsel Drive, P.O. Box 669, Mankato, Minnesota 56002
http://www.capstone-press.com

1 2 3 4 5 6 06 05 04 03 02 01

Library of Congress Cataloging-in-Publication Data
Frost, Helen, 1949–
        What are inclined planes? / by Helen Frost.
        p. cm.—(Looking at simple machines)
        Includes bibliographical references (p. 23) and index.
        ISBN 0-7368-0845-0
        1. Inclined planes—Juvenile literature. [1. Inclined planes.] I.Title. II. Series.
TJ147 .F76 2001
621.8′11—dc21

00-009866

Summary: Simple text and photographs present inclined planes and their function as
a simple machine.

Note to Parents and Teachers

The Looking at Simple Machines series supports national science
standards for units on understanding work, force, and tools. This
book describes inclined planes and illustrates how they make work
easier. The photographs support early readers in understanding
the text. This book also introduces early readers to subject-specific
vocabulary words, which are defined in the Words to Know section.
Early readers may need assistance to read some words and to use
the Table of Contents, Words to Know, Read More, Internet Sites,
and Index/Word List sections of the book.

Table of Contents

inclined plane

4

An inclined plane is
a simple machine. An
inclined plane is a slope.

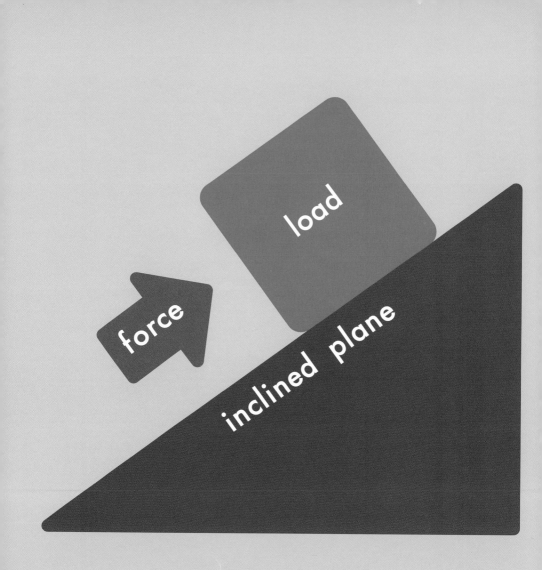

A force moves a load up an inclined plane.

An inclined plane makes work easier.

force

Lifting a heavy load is hard.

force

Moving a heavy load
up an inclined plane
is easier.

A load also can move
down an inclined plane.

A ramp is
an inclined plane.

Stairs are
an inclined plane.

A slide is
an inclined plane.

Words to Know

force—a push or a pull on an object; force makes objects start moving, speed up, change direction, or stop moving.

inclined plane—a sloping surface that is a simple machine; an inclined plane makes it easier to raise and lower heavy loads.

load—an object that is carried or lifted

ramp—a surface that slants to connect two levels

simple machine—a tool that makes work easier; an inclined plane is a simple machine; screws and wedges are simple machines that use inclined planes.

slope—a slanted surface; one end is higher than the other end on a slope.

stairs—a group of steps between two levels; stairs are a bumpy inclined plane.

work—using a force to move an object across a distance

Read More

Armentrout, Patricia. *The Inclined Plane.* Simple Devices. Vero Beach, Fla.: Rourke, 1997.

Oxlade, Chris. *Machines.* Young Scientist Concepts and Projects. Milwaukee: Gareth Stevens, 1998.

Rush, Caroline. *Slopes.* Simple Science. Austin, Texas: Raintree Steck-Vaughn, 1997.

Welsbacher, Anne. *Inclined Planes.* Understanding Simple Machines. Mankato, Minn.: Bridgestone Books, 2001.

Internet Sites

Inclined Planes
http://www.brainpop.com/tech/simplemachines/inclinedplane/index.weml

Simple Machines
http://www.fi.edu/qa97/spotlight3/spotlight3.html

What Is an Inclined Plane?
http://www.professorbeaker.com/plane_fact.html

Index/Word List

down, 15
easier, 9, 13
force, 7
hard, 11
heavy, 11, 13
lifting, 11
load, 7, 11, 13, 15
machine, 5

move, 7, 13, 15
ramp, 17
simple, 5
slide, 21
slope, 5
stairs, 19
up, 7, 13
work, 9

Word Count: 70
Early-Intervention Level: 9

Editorial Credits
Martha E. H. Rustad, editor; Kia Bielke, cover designer and illustrator; Kimberly Danger, photo researcher

Photo Credits
David F. Clobes, 10, 12, 14, 16
Index Stock Imagery, 20
Photo Network/T.J. Florian, cover
Unicorn Stock Photos/Chromosohm/Joe Sohm, 1
Visuals Unlimited/John Sohlden, 8; Mark E. Gibson, 18

The author thanks the children's section staff at the Allen County Public Library in Fort Wayne, Indiana, for research assistance. The author also thanks Josué Njock Libii, Ph.D, Associate Professor of Mechanical Engineering at Indiana University–Purdue University in Fort Wayne, Indiana.

24